Sad Clown Paradox

Rosh Abdullah

to curtis
thank you

smell ya later

contents

funny

flex

why do real estate agents
put a *sold* sign over the *for sale* sign
can't you just take away the whole sign altogether

no, the people must know
see this gold jacket?
i am good at what i do

hazardous parrots

the only time we use the word *flesh*
is in porn or dystopian novels
to describe viruses that eat our skin

the only time we use the word *exotic*
is to describe women from countries we can't spell
and birds with feathers of more than one colour

why is that?

celebrities without makeup

where do all the unsold magazines go
once the month is up
and the new issues are in

i know they don't give it to the homeless
like leftover donuts and bagels
can you imagine
giving people with no money
tabloids about millionaires

they're just like us
that's why it's called us weekly

i guess they toss them in the bin
every first of the month
which seems like a waste
until you realize
that's where they belong

that's why it's called trash mag

                              and i think that's really beautiful
i really admire
when toilet paper has designs
like flowers and hearts
printed on it
because each quilt knows their purpose
born to wipe the shit from my asshole

and still they rise

if someone yells
show us your tits
just show us your tits
we will really appreciate it
and we've had a very long day
we are tired and just want to see some tits before bed
and then we'll stop
we promise

we'll also say they are nice
even if we don't think they are

it is a very vulnerable position we are in
if you want to talk status
we have none

most of you are very rude
when you don't want to show us the tits
so we're taking a huge chance here
because you might yell back

brené brown says to be brave
so let's both be brave
and pull 'em out, love

let's have a lookie then

cherry blossoms

last summer
i went to the park during cherry blossom season
and there was a fence around the blossoms
and security detail nearby
making sure no one got too close
and i don't think i should have to ask this

but what the fuck did we do that we can't be trusted around trees?

or what did the trees do that they can't be trusted around us?

pride

june is a great month
there are rainbow flags everywhere
and all the banks are gay now

good for them
good for you, bmo
so brave

but where do all the rainbow flags go
once june is over
suddenly banks become college kids
when parents visit dorm rooms

get rid of the empties
hide the bong
take down that flag

i mean, it's not like my bank
to capitalize on something for profit
they even put it on their website
love is love

but if do i think about it
i guess from july-may
the login page does say
no homo

wealth

i've heard it said a lot
that money is evil
so i guess it's a good thing
the richest people only make up 1% of the population

can you imagine the danger
if more people had that kind of money

petting zoo

as a society
we have deemed it
not weird
when children are turned on
by sexy cartoon animals

like lola bunny from space jam
or roxanne from a goofy movie

it is ok
for kids to have a sexual awakening
as long as it's anthropomorphic
because now it is wholesome

we do not draw the line
at underage turtles with six packs
but what we won't tolerate
is any other type
of sexual confusion

burn her

i think it's funny we call it a *witch hunt*
that implies we had a chance to run

or the *salem witch trials*
which makes it sound like
there was investigative work involved
when really it was just people yelling
she's a witch
at any woman they felt wronged by

how long do you think those trials lasted?

your honour, we'd like to present exhibit a
this slightly eccentric hat she sometimes wears

but men were allowed to wear funny hats in the 1690s
because, you know
not all warlocks

i stopped trusting people
once i discovered what circumcisions were

because somebody looked at a baby's penis
and their first thought was
some of that's gotta go

curse

when the doctor asks
if i'm sexually active
i don't break eye contact

i'm celibate
but not by choice
i didn't forward a chain email seven years ago

it said this would happen

raise a glass
to the bride and groom
a tuxedo man toasts

i entertain the idea
of holding up my divacup
next to their champagne flutes

but i stop myself
no, not here
they wouldn't get it

big fish

it's easy to be a big shot here
when the most famous person
is the kid down the street
with an autoimmune disorder
who got their name in the paper last year

thank god they didn't die
or else everyone would've forgotten about me

i don't care if eggs raise my cholesterol levels
where are the scientific studies
about former leash kids

i just want to know
if they're super kinky now

twist

not a lot of people know this
but m. night shyamalan
co-wrote the screenplay for stuart little (1999)

when i remind people that
it surprises them
but it shouldn't
because if you recall in the movie
the littles try to find stuart's biological parents
and they show up to take stuart back
but later we find out
that stuart's parents
have been dead the entire time

classic shyamalan

when i have a cupcake
or a slice of pizza
i try to pick the biggest slice
or the cupcake with the most frosting

but when i go to those seafood restaurants
where they let you pick your own lobster
i try to pick the one that looks least likely
to have a family that will miss him

maybe that's why people
put photos of their family
in their wallets
so when people rob them
they don't also get murdered

someone should check the statistics
of murder victims
who have photos of people
in their wallets
versus people whose wallets
have photos of their cats

because i think i can guess
which number is higher

civilization

sometimes historians on tv
will say things like
as you can see
the drawings on the vase
are painted in red
which symbolizes fertility
and a bountiful crop year

but sometimes i wonder
if maybe it's red
because the only paint they had
was blood

incognito mode

it's ironic to me
that in every alcoholics anonymous meeting
everyone reveals their name
to the entire room

that's one hell of a trust fall

i wonder if they do the same thing
in narcotics anonymous
even though it has *narc* in the name

merit badge

if you think about it
the best candidate
to teach knot tying
to a bunch of boy scouts
is a leather daddy

and if you really think about it
the best candidate
to be a leather daddy
is a scoutmaster

ode to the shower cry

it is safe lying naked
in this porcelain hug
no one out there has a clue
to what's going on
but we know the hurt
so stay as long as you need
there's no judgement here
no one watches you bleed

it's international waters, baby
cry
sob
wail
go ahead and scream
it's your hilary duff moment
time to come clean

what was once a rusty showerhead
is now your trusted exorcist
spraying holy water
from his unholy crucifix
disinfecting the wounds
yes, it should feel like burning
projectile crying is good
that just means it's working

bathing in that good gospel
and feeling reborn
when suddenly there's a knock
on the bathroom door

it's your roommate
he's concerned
hey, man
you okay?

you think quickly
yeah, all good
just singing some kanye

you sure?
he asks
'cause it sounds like you're crying

yeah, i'm fine
you maintain the circle jerk lying

alright, cool
he leaves without saying goodbye
you return to your breakdown
now, where was i?

and when the whole thing is over
and you're a margin less bruised
no need to thank us
we'll just meet you back here
the next time raptors lose

hibernate

ah, winter
can't live with it
can't write your unauthorized steve irwin musical without it

the real 5 stages of grief

1. weed
2. carbs
3. a rabbit vibrator
4. your downstairs neighbours
   politely asking if you can turn down
   or play something other than adele
5. every movie starring timothée chalamet
   (can be combined with stage 3. extra points if crying)

pagliacci

if you can't handle me at my self-published book of amateur poetry
then you don't deserve me at my improv show comp ticket
valued at ten dollars

fun get-to-know-you questions to ask on a first date
1. which primary colour has wronged you the most in your life?
2. do you prefer to eat hot dogs inside the bun or outside your boss's apartment?
3. in a zombie apocalypse, would you use turbotax or h&r block?
4. do you think it's the carrot or the top hat that makes a snowman so sexy?
5. if you won the lottery, do you think you are statistically more or less likely to get lyme disease?
6. what's the last satanic message you heard when you watched a sunnyd commercial backwards?
7. if you only had one more day to live, would you call them *overalls* or *dungarees*?
8. sex, marry, kill. which one do you think a viking likes most?
9. what's your favourite song to tie your shoes to?
10. where do you keep your baby teeth?

not
funny

i told you that word, in norwegian
with the fire, inside at christmas
that is the word
we think means *cozy*, or *warm*
but i know it means
lying between you and her, naked
sleeping until someone says *that's enough*
it won't be her
because she is cozy
but you are the fire
you are warm

advice

when someone is sad
we tell them it is better to have loved and lost
when someone is happy
we say ignorance is bliss

well, which is it?

every heart has their version of
if that i endured
then surely this too

although we've forgotten
the degree of hurt
we know it's there
under the skin
flesh memory
watch what happens when it returns
it will return

and you will see
the greatest survival response we have
is how quickly we forget
how badly we wanted to die

my mother once said
she believes hell is here on earth

if that's true
then it may not be a system of punishment
just a circumstance of endurance

and if we've built the hero's journey
and all morals of this world
on *good* versus *evil*
then *purpose* and *penalty*
are second cousins
once removed

but *fluke* and *doom*
they are brothers

ants

we are not nothing
because we are insignificant
we are nothing
because we are insignificant
and that makes us important

the catch-22 of immigrant parents

when you visit
they ask you
to help with a hundred little things
like make calls to banks
and insurance companies
because they don't understand
and are convinced
their english isn't good enough

we're too young
to be parents
parenting our parents

so you stop visiting
the ones who gave you life

but then you forget
and you miss them
and the food
that you know you won't taste again
after they die
at least, not the way she makes it
which is the best way

so you go back
and after you eat
the sixteen course meal
they ask you to help
with a hundred big things
damage control
for all the blunders they made
when they tried to do it themselves

and you get annoyed
that they didn't wait for you
so you could've done it right
the first time

you ask them why they tried
when they know they don't understand
and their english isn't good enough

and they look at you, scared
the ones who gave you life
when they try to explain

the last time we asked
you got mad
and stopped coming

and it's then you realize
they think you're only here for the meal

goldilocks

the best advice
my mom ever gave me
was right before i went to university

she told me
don't marry the first man you meet
fall in love
get your heart broken
and then fall in love again
so that you know

more than one person can make you happy

when things were good
is when i would ask
in what ways isn't it?
and feel so much shame
i'd need to shower

but i knew
it couldn't be that
because that glorified hat stand
makes me want to vomit

well, i figured it out
smoking weed in the sun
feeling clean
lying in the dirt

when things were bad
i still asked
in what ways isn't it?

last words

if i saw your face on the street
i wouldn't say *hi*
but i know what i'd say

square in the eyes
i'd tell you straight

you weren't good to me
and if i have to explain to you why
then you're still the same person

a eulogy

when i heard there was another girl
another victim
i'm happy to say it gave me closure

oh, i thought
it had nothing to do with me

i did nothing wrong
i just happened to have a ponytail
and he was the ponytail slasher

(condolences to her and the family)

gaslight anthem

for the little girl
scared of the con
tell the matchstick man
that you're not wrong

no one calls me a whore
more than my dad
and no one means it less than him

if you make a joke
you have to say *just kidding* after
or *jk,* for a youthful flair
otherwise no one will laugh
and it kills the vibe

but if you do tell people you're joking
then everyone knows you don't mean it
even if it is mean

and then it's funny
do you get it?

cardboard box

they used to sell mixtapes on the tv
i never want to forget that

i thought it was dumb at the time
but it wasn't the cd's fault
that was on me
for not having a sense of humour

maybe i made the greatest mistake of my life
when i left our home
maybe what i think it should be
doesn't exist
or maybe it does
but not for me

the only way this could be right
is if it works out for one of us
it doesn't have to be me
but my god
i hope it's you

it has to be you
because i'm such a clichéd sinner
and you deserve the world

so i'll wait for that call
when you ring me up and say
i understand now

why that had to end
so that this could happen
and be truly happy

until i get that call
i'll sit here thinking
maybe i made the greatest mistake of our lives

expert

ten thousand hours of loving you
made me a goddess

mark ruffalo doesn't do it for me anymore

i don't know why
but it feels wrong to imagine
my former partner while masturbating

maybe it's because i didn't get permission
even though it's only imaginary
or maybe it feels like an insult
to the breakup process

and it would be rude to picture someone else
i mean, it only just happened

so instead i try to imagine a made-up person
maybe someone i am assigned to populate mars with
but i can't picture another human being of interest
i can't even imagine my vibrator wearing a mustache

so i masturbate to the thought of no one
which makes it all very unsexy
and difficult to come to
i still do
but it's not great

and after it's done
i think to myself
one day i'll touch myself
to the thought of someone real
and then i try to imagine who it could be

but i can't

i have no more sad to give
i spent it all
the last of it i used
on spotify premium

and now i can't be sad
even if it's time
because i have no more sad to give

if i do somehow find a bit
lost in some pocket
from a jacket i haven't worn since last winter
stuffed inside a used, crumpled tissue
and i use it now, on you
i will disintegrate
there won't be anything of me left
and then i really will
have no more sad to give

if i sit on my parents' sofa
which is more like a sister to me these days
and i hear the jingling between seats
cram my hand in that cushioned cranny
and pull out some loose pieces
just enough for one last go
i'll need to save it
for when i really need it
an emergency
like to watch *eternal sunshine* on valentine's day
i'll need it then
so that i don't disintegrate

so i must go gentle now

calm, calm is my new requisite disposition
because, and i can't stress this enough
but i've no more sad to give

so that's why i can't make it to book club this week

sportmate

sometimes when i'm lonely
and i think
what's the point of it all
i tell myself
i am someone's person
and they are waiting for me

and then i think
i wonder if someone else
was their person before me
but then they died
so coach sent me in

and then i realize
i've probably lost my starters too

which means
my alternates
are other people's first picks
that i've been stealing

so if you think about it
we're all someone's substitute
in an endless draft cycle

this entire time
we've been waiting for *the one*
when we never really had a soulmate at all

just benchwarmers

single

am i too much?

no,
says everyone who won't date me

superposition

i am not the star of this universe
i think i'm in the wrong parallel

i can't be sure
but i don't know if heroes are supposed to cry
when putting on their face serums
it doesn't make for a great montage

not everyone knows my name
not everyone read this book

my best friend is in love
maybe i'm in her world
there's no way to confirm it
but i don't think there's a 50/50 chance

i'm afraid the cat is straight up dead

koinophobia

i have a fear of being mediocre
i don't know if you can relate
but i have a fear of being mediocre
that keeps me from being great

my biggest fear
is a *deathbed yes*

in that last breath
i'll know the answer
between the only two possibles
to the same two questions
asked in different ways
like those recipes
eggplant parm
two ways
ask it as different as you like
two ways
same meal

i'm terrified of the waiter
coming to the table
at the end of the meal, asking
how was everything
and me thinking
should have ordered the carbonara

glory

sometimes i wonder
which would i prefer
to achieve the height of legacy
posthumously
never knowing the impact
or dying a happy nobody

it sounds obvious, right?

girl crush

alone in my room
lying on my bed
listening to my playlist
girls rule, boys drool
while reading poetry
and scribbling thoughts
in the margins

16-year-old me
is stoked to turn 28
and be doing the same old shit

except now i have tattoos
hell yeah

masterpiece

i produce my greatest work
without a muse
because alone
i can be a piece of shit

and isn't that an artist in her prime?

sad clown paradox

if i make a joke in the woods
and no one is around to laugh

am i still funny?

you know those punishments
in greek mythology

like how sisyphus has to roll that boulder up a hill
for all of time
because it keeps rolling down
every time he reaches the top
(he's still going at it, by the way)

or when prometheus gave people *fire*
so zeus chained him to a rock
and sent an eagle to eat out his liver
and every night his liver would grow back
and this was supposed to go on for eternity

yeah, that's what depression feels like
a cruel and dramatic punishment
that will last forever

except i have no idea
why the gods feel slighted
maybe it's for something i haven't done yet
future karma, possibly
but if there's no such thing
then their sense of retribution is a joke
like using a monkey's paw
to wish for rapture
then getting the end times

when i said i wanted to go somewhere warm
i didn't mean hell
but here we are every december
at an all-inclusive elephants' graveyard
where self-esteem and libidos go to die

there is nothing more homicidal
barring the actual act of murder
than being forced to make chit-chat
in a beige building with someone
whose name i'm only 42% confident i know
having to answer
about what i'm doing this weekend
which is the same thing
i'm doing right now
just trying to hold it together, janet
or susan
i don't know
and i don't fucking care

how come no one stands by the water cooler, saying
everydays, am i right?
bring back the grumpy tv husband trope
so that people can find me hilarious again

and of course i've considered it
this isn't amateur hour at the apollo
but if i kill myself
someone still has to pay my student loans
and i might be boring
but i'm not an asshole

so what do you say
to heal a rock bottom

in the rests and betweens
the breaths before the boulder push
the nights the liver regenerates
in those infinite meantimes
i can only sigh and tell myself

use
it
in
your
art,
i
guess

9 781999 543525